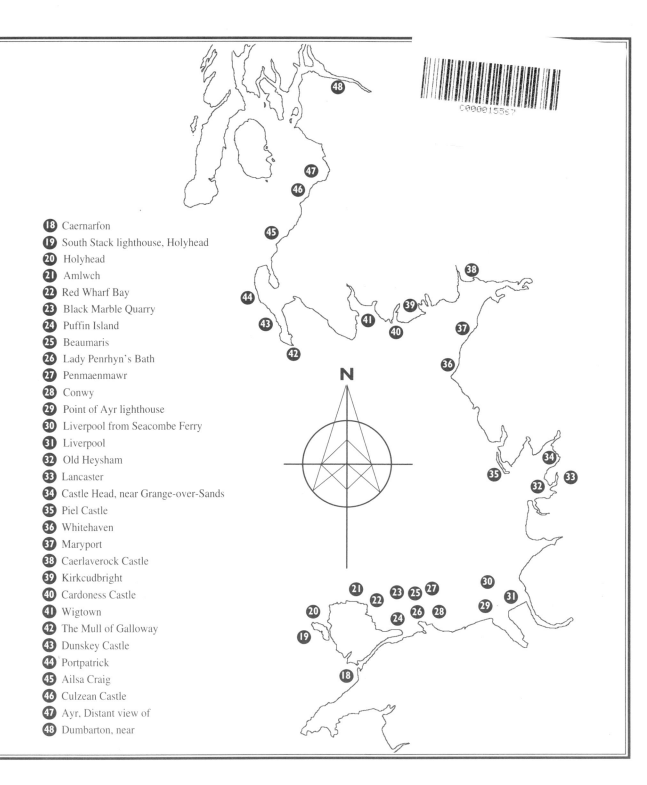

18 Caernarfon
19 South Stack lighthouse, Holyhead
20 Holyhead
21 Amlwch
22 Red Wharf Bay
23 Black Marble Quarry
24 Puffin Island
25 Beaumaris
26 Lady Penrhyn's Bath
27 Penmaenmawr
28 Conwy
29 Point of Ayr lighthouse
30 Liverpool from Seacombe Ferry
31 Liverpool
32 Old Heysham
33 Lancaster
34 Castle Head, near Grange-over-Sands
35 Piel Castle
36 Whitehaven
37 Maryport
38 Caerlaverock Castle
39 Kirkcudbright
40 Cardoness Castle
41 Wigtown
42 The Mull of Galloway
43 Dunskey Castle
44 Portpatrick
45 Ailsa Craig
46 Culzean Castle
47 Ayr, Distant view of
48 Dumbarton, near

N

A VOYAGE
ROUND GREAT BRITAIN

Volume 2

Land's End to the Clyde

For Nicholas and Susan

A VOYAGE ROUND GREAT BRITAIN

Volume 2
Land's End to the Clyde

by

David Addey

in the footsteps of William Daniell R.A.
(1769-1837)

SPELLMOUNT

Staplehurst

British Library Cataloguing in Publication Data:
A catalogue record for this book is available
from the British Library

Copyright © David Addey 1997

Foreword © Melvyn Bragg 1997

ISBN 1-873376-97-9

First published in the UK in 1997 by
Spellmount Limited
The Old Rectory
Staplehurst
Kent TN12 0AZ

1 3 5 7 9 8 6 4 2

Typeset in 11/12 Baskerville by
MATS, Southend-on-Sea, Essex

Printed in Hong Kong

GENERAL NOTE

Daniell's exploration of the coast began at Land's End in 1813 in the company of his friend, Richard Ayton. He probably arrived at Dumbarton in 1816 having parted company with Ayton soon after entering Scotland.

The text to the Daniell aquatints was written by Ayton until they reached Scotland, thereafter it was written by Daniell. Apart from one or two minor amendments, the extracts are reproduced in their own words. The spelling of certain names and words that were in common use at the beginning of the 19th century has been retained.

The first two stages of my Voyage, from Sheerness to Land's End, had been completed by the time I arrived at Land's End on 14th September 1990. The seventy-four scenes depicted up to then were published in 1995.

I continued my Voyage from Land's End in the autumn of 1991 and reached Dumbarton on 19th September 1994.

ACKNOWLEDGMENTS

The tragic death in July 1991 of my dear wife Shirley brought an end to thirty-four years of constant devotion and support. The progress which my Voyage has made since then has been due entirely to the encouragement received from many friends and strangers, for which I am most grateful. Again, I have often been provided with food and shelter in the course of my travels, and access to all the sites selected by Daniell has been freely granted.

My account of the first two stages of the Voyage was published in 1995, and I would like to thank Jamie Wilson of Spellmount Ltd. for his interest and care in producing the first volume of this project.

Previously, I had the invaluable assistance of John Henderson, who enjoyed supplying a turn of phrase or just the word that I was looking for but could not find. Sadly, he passed away before this work had been completed, and I would like to pay tribute to his knowledge, enthusiasm and kindness.

My thanks to Peter Humphreys of Wells Graphics for his skill in the photography of the paintings, and also to friends and strangers, museums, information bureaux and other organisations without whose help it would have been impossible to fill in a number of gaps in my research.

FOREWORD

Comparing the past with the present is a popular pastime, guaranteed, as few other things are, to favour the elderly. This is very useful in a society wearily worshipping youth.

Comparing the present with the past in ways which can be pinned down – unlike the delicious hot air of 'golden ages' – is a serious business and here we have a very good chance to see it in action.

Starting 175 years ago William Daniell and Richard Ayton sailed round the British Isles and painted much of what they saw. David Addey has done the same in recent years.

The comparison between the two periods of time, between two locations both similar and dissimilar and between the brief descriptions of the places is a rich source of pleasure artistically and historically.

Here we can see – literally see – the changes in a social landscape which brought us to where we are today.

Sometimes the entries are very poignant, Whitehaven for instance, a town I know well on the west coast of Cumbria, is seen in all its greatness by Daniell and Ayton when it was the third port in England. Now the ship building and the 204 vessels which once belonged to the port are utterly gone. And, like so many of Britain's depleted centres of industrial strength and excellence, it is fighting to discover a new future for itself.

Many people baffled by the sensations of current British art will find here evidence of what is a continuing though largely unsung strain of British artists' long love of and loving depiction of a landscape. We are rich in topographical water-colourists. Here Daniell, Ayton and Addey take us from Land's End to the Clyde, the rugged most Celtic, western coast once thought to be at the farthest edge of the known world.

Melvyn Bragg
October 1997

INTRODUCTION

In 1812 William Daniell and Richard Ayton set out from Land's End with the intention of circumnavigating the British Isles in a boat. Daniell, at the age of only 17, had already travelled extensively in India with his uncle, Thomas Daniell. On their return in 1794 they published their 'Oriental Scenery', an enormous work in six volumes comprising 144 coloured aquatints. The last of the six was published in 1808, a year after William had been elected an Associate of the Royal Academy. He was elected a full Academician in 1822.

When in 1996 a number of the Daniells' watercolours of India were sold at auction in London for prices ranging from £1,000 to £91,000, their reputation as competent topographical artists was firmly established.

The Daniell family lived at Chertsey. Thomas's father was the landlord of the Swan Inn and was succeeded by Thomas's elder brother, William, and his wife, Sarah. They had two sons, William (1769) and Samuel (1775) who was also an artist. He worked in South Africa and Ceylon and died in Ceylon at the early age of thirty-seven.

In 1801 William Daniell married Mary Westall, the elder sister of the artists, Richard and Michael Westall. They had four daughters; three of them married but remained childless. The eldest of the four died at the old Daniell home at Chertsey in 1912, in her 103rd year.

One asks oneself how the idea of the Voyage Round Great Britain was conceived and planned. A vast amount of travelling was involved over a span of ten years, not only along the coast but also in journeying from Chertsey and back again. Moreover, it seems likely that Sarah Daniell would have had to bring up the four children very largely on her own. There were none of the modern amenities that we take for granted today, but perhaps life was lived at a more leisurely pace.

The idea that I should follow in Daniell's footsteps was suggested to me by Martyn Gregory, the London fine art dealer and, in the late summer of 1988, I set out from Sheerness in north Kent. Travelling in a clockwise direction I reached Land's End in September 1990. Like Daniell, I have not worked continuously on this project; it seems that he did not travel for four of the ten years. Similarly, I have generally travelled on my Voyage in alternate years.

Thomas and William Daniell had mastered the art of the aquatint, and William reproduced the 308 coastal scenes in eight volumes with a comprehensive text. Regrettably, many of these volumes were later broken up and today you rarely find a complete set. On the other hand the Tate Gallery acquired the original copper plates, and in 1978 a limited edition of the engravings was published, accompanied by Daniell's complete text and illustrations, in two volumes. I was lucky enough to find and purchase a set of engravings, together with the text.

Daniell's aquatints were all produced to the same size, 165mm by 237mm (6½″ × 9½″) and hand-coloured by professional colourists. The process of the aquatint was specially successful in the representation of watercolour washes, while the etched line is still used for features such as the masts and rigging of ships or details of buildings. Originally introduced from the Continent by Paul Sandby (1725-1809), the technique was perfected by the Daniells.

Daniell travelled mainly in the summer months whereas I have preferred the spring and autumn. Our approach to the work differs slightly: Daniell sketched and then engraved, whereas I produce a finished drawing on the spot which is later coloured in the studio.

BIBLIOGRAPHY

Addey, David — *A Voyage Round Great Britain, Sheerness to Land's End.* Spellmount Ltd., Staplehurst, 1995

Caernarvonshire Historical Society — Transactions No. 36 (1975). Pages 124–129

Daniell, William and Richard Ayton — *A Voyage Round Great Britain.* The 1977 edition with notes, published by the Tate Gallery Publications Dept.

Drive Publications Ltd. — *Illustrated Guide to Britain's Coast.* The Reader's Digest Association Ltd., 1984

Ellis, Sheila — *Down a Cobbled Street.* The story of Clovelly, Badger Books, Bideford, 1987

Moore, Donald — *Artists' View of Glamorgan.* Glamorgan Archive Service, Cardiff and Swansea, 1988

Mark R Myers and Michael Nix — *Hartland Quay, The story of a Vanished Port.* Hartland Quay Museum, 1982

Sale, Evans and McLean — *Walking Britain's Coast – an aerial guide.* Unwin Hyman Ltd., 1989

Somerville, Christopher — *Coastal Walks in England and Wales.* Grafton Books, 1988

Steele P. — *Beaumaris, the town's story.* Magma Books, 1996

Stubbs, Arthur — *A Brief History of Tenby Harbour and Surrounding Area.* 1994

Sutton, Thomas — *The Daniells, Artists and Travellers.* Theodore Brun, 1954

Break, break, break,
   On thy cold gray stones, O Sea!
And I would that my tongue could utter
   The thoughts that arise in me.

O well for the fisherman's boy
   That he shouts with his sister at play!
O well for the sailor lad,
   That he sings in his boat on the bay!

And the stately ships go on
   To their haven under the hill;
But O for the touch of a vanish'd hand
   And the sound of a voice that is still!

Break, break, break,
   At the foot of thy crags, O Sea!
But the tender grace of a day that is dead
   Will never come back to me.

Alfred, Lord Tennyson

1 LAND'S END

The reader will find the two navigators frequently sailing on horseback or scudding in a gig and it is necessary to explain the causes which obliged them to prosecute their course by means so irregular and unfamiliar. When the undertaking of circumnavigating the coast was first designed it was intended to travel principally by sea in a small rowing boat but, on experiment, the plan was found to be utterly impractical. Rapid tides, ground swells, insurmountable surfs, strong winds and foul winds are among the catalogue of horrors on the coast, which were frequently raging all at the same time, none of which could be encountered with safety in a small boat.

1 LAND'S END

. . . a year has passed since I reached Land's End after completing the second stage of my 'Voyage': the foreboding that I felt at that time had become a dreadful reality with the death of my wife in July 1991. The 'Voyage' was now a lifeline, and with deep emotion I returned to Land's End where we had stood together a year earlier, wrapped in our love and our own private thoughts about the future . . .

. . . .

Until they reached Combe Martin in north Devon, this view, which is from Whitesand Bay, together with a close-up view of the Longships lighthouse, are the only scenes depicted by Daniell from the boat in which he and Ayton had embarked at Land's End; tempestuous weather had brought an early end to their plans to sail round the coast.

2 PORTREATH

Portreath has a few small houses, scattered about in a valley between two lofty hills, and is scarcely to be dignified with the name of a town, for it has no pretensions to a street and in very few instances has one house adjoining another. It is, nevertheless, a place of considerable bustle and business and has a harbour, which is always crowded with vessels. The entrance to the harbour is singularly frightful and has an air of preposterousness and grotesque expediency about it, very striking to those who have always considered a harbour as obviously presenting a place of shelter and security for ships. In bad weather a vessel goes through a most tremendous trial when approaching it, for she comes within two or three yards of rocks, which if she touches she is lost.

2 PORTREATH

The 'bustle and business' of the village has disappeared and only a few fishing boats and pleasure craft remain. The pier was built in 1760 and the harbour thrived on the export of copper and tin and the import of coal. Coasters visited the harbour until the 1960s but trade has now ceased and the surrounding land has been developed as a residential estate. A feature that still remains is the beacon on the cliff.

Although Daniell and Ayton visited St Ives, which they found to be 'neat and decent' with a large harbour, a view of the town is not included in their 'Voyage'. Similarly, there is no view of Port Isaac where they 'were assailed by an indescribable stench', which made them hasten from the village in a 'transport of disgust'.

3 BOSCASTLE

The harbour at Portreath is very frightful but the crookedness of the channel at Boscastle is the cause of many difficulties; the most serious is the contrariety of the wind, which may be fair in one reach and foul in another, and thus occasion, in so narrow a passage, extreme confusion in the steerage of the vessel and the management of her sails. The pier is very small but it forms a pretty line, which is very picturesque in itself, and harmonizes with the form of the objects about it.

3 BOSCASTLE

The harbour, now in the care of the National Trust, has hardly changed since Daniell's visit. While I was walking along the rock face on the north side of the harbour, the small box in which I carry my materials flew open and, in horror, I watched the contents slither into the water. I managed to scramble down and rescue most of the items but not before I had been saturated by a freak wave.

4 HARTLAND QUAY

Hartland Quay consists of a cluster of mean cottages, which have no evident comfort about them. The situation of the village is more than commonly rude and romantic; to the right and left extends the coast in a line of towering cliffs of black rock; in front is a little harbour, marked out and secured by a semicircular pier.

This was the first place that we had paused, during the course of our voyage, where there was no provision for strangers; we had surprised many hotels that were in a very doubtful state of extremity, but here was one still holding out a promise of entertainment, but in all its parts absolutely defunct. There was, however, a great spirit of hospitality in the landlord which sufficed to appease us; for, as Dr Johnson observes, where there is yet shame, there may in time be virtue.

4 HARTLAND QUAY

The weather had deteriorated severely by the time I reached Hartland Quay, and this was the first occasion that I had witnessed the fury of the Atlantic as it tore into the small bay. I was more fortunate than Ayton and Daniell in that one of the 'mean cottages' is now a public house and I was able to shelter there until the storm had abated. Very little remains of the 16th century pier depicted by Daniell and which had been a refuge on this inhospitable coast for many years. The rock formations in the cliffs, which go from horizontal to vertical in the space of a few metres, are particularly impressive. Lundy Island is shown in Daniell's view, but I was unable to see it through the spray and low cloud.

5 CLOVELLY

The town of Clovelly is built on the aclivity of a steep hill and when seen from the bottom the houses have a most singular appearance, rising step by step, with the roof of one house below the base of another. There are some disadvantages from this mode of building, amongst which I particularly noticed that the chimneys of the lower houses regularly vomit forth their smoke into the parlour windows of those above them. In labouring up or sliding down the steep steps of the town, one ought to possess the lungs and legs of a Welsh pony, to travel with any degree of comfort or security. At Clovelly a man cannot step up to chat with a neighbour a cloud or two above him, without expending more breath in the journey than would be sufficient for an hour's walk, so that if not very longwinded he must give up all hope of long stories.

5 CLOVELLY

The Red Lion Hotel, situated at the shore end of the pier, became my base for a few days and it was from here that this view was drawn. Little has changed since Daniell's visit except that the balcony on the cottage by the beach has been extended. It is the cottage with the balcony in Daniell's view that is known as 'Crazy Kate's'. Kate Lyall would watch her husband from an upper window as he fished in the bay but, one day, he was drowned before her eyes and she became demented. She never recovered and died in 1736.

In 1821 and 1838 there were two terrible fishing disasters when a total of fifty-two fishermen lost their lives. A little fishing still takes place, but the village, with its steep, narrow cobbled streets, now thrives as a major tourist attraction.

6 ILFRACOMBE

Ilfracombe has an excellent harbour, easy of access, yet secured against any injurious effects of wind and sea. The bason of the harbour is surrounded on three sides by the land, and on the fourth is protected from the north or sea-wind by a bold mass of rock which stretches nearly half way across the mouth. On the summit of this rock, which rises pyramidally, is erected a lighthouse for the direction of ships in the night. The lighthouse is built in the form of a chapel, a whimsical fancy that has treated 'the genius of the place' rather too cavalierly. No one would think of fixing a chapel of ease, really dedicated to the users of a chapel, on the top of a high, steep, rugged rock.

6 ILFRACOMBE, LANTERN HILL

There has been little change to this view, where the Chapel of St Nicholas has burnt a guiding light for mariners for over 600 years. The rise and fall of the tide here is the second highest in the world; the greatest variation occurs in the Bay of Funday in Newfoundland, while that in the United Kingdom is at Minehead in Somerset.

7 ILFRACOMBE FROM HILSBOROUGH

From the church, the town extends to the sea-side, in one street about a mile in length, of suitable breadth, well paved and remarkably clean. As nearly the whole town is included in this one street it is almost superfluous to observe that the houses are built without any respect for regularity. The tinker is of course a window narrower and a storey lower than the baker, who in his turn is overtopped by the butcher, while all crouch, in due subordination, under the tower of the doctor. But in spite of this gradation of ranks, the general appearance of the town is very respectable, and to our eyes that had not of late been accustomed to palaces, the street, with its shops and pavement, looked quite metropolitan.

7 ILFRACOMBE FROM HILLSBOROUGH

A fine view is obtained from this hill which rises to the east of the town. The advent of the railway brought tourists flocking to this elegant 19th-century holiday resort which, for many years, had been a busy harbour and a safe haven on an inhospitable stretch of coast. The pier promenade at the foot of Lantern Hill was built in 1872 and served the steamers that sailed from Bristol and South Wales. The spire of Holy Trinity parish church is in the middle distance of my view.

Daniell has moved Lundy Island so that the whole of it can be seen but only its north end is visible from the hill. On my visit it was obscured by a low sea mist.

8 NEAR COMBMARTIN

The little inlet is fully occupied by a few boats on the beach, and by a group of cottages beyond. We found that one of the cottages was a public house, with no promise on the outside. but furnished with plenty within, and a very sensible landlady, who maintained that nothing was superior to a good breakfast, which she regarded as the foundation on which every thing useful or agreeable in the business of the day was to be raised. We were precisely in a state to coincide with her opinion, and to admit, that no circumstances, however elevated, can make us forget, for any length of time, that we have a stomach. In five minutes all the male population of the village had assembled about us at our meal; and, ale, a great leveller, soon determined that there should be no secrets between us.

8 NEAR COMBE MARTIN

In a project such as this, an important aspect is accommodation, coupled with good food. From time to time I stay with friends or in small but comfortable hotels, but the majority of nights are spent in bed and breakfasts. Occasionally, the single male is treated with suspicion and not made welcome, particularly when he occupies a double room which could earn more money. The breakfasts, though, are served in much the same way as they were for Daniell and Ayton, with enough sustenance to last a whole day.

Since their departure from Land's End, this was the first view that Daniell had depicted from a boat. It really is necessary to approach Combe Martin by sea in order to appreciate the dramatic scenery, dominated by Great Hangman, which is the highest point on the South West Peninsula Way.

9 LYNMOUTH

At Lynmouth there is an opening in the cliffs, and through this there unexpectedly dawns upon you a view of the interior very limited indeed in extent, but varied and picturesque, and a little village in the place of the rude rocks at the water's edge. This scene was suddenly disclosed to us, after gazing at the blank rocks, like the glitter and show of the stage, by the drawing up of the curtain at a theatre. But the most imposing feature in the prospect is a huge, rugged, and barren mountain in the background. We had intended to make Lynmouth the boundary of our day's voyage, but discovered that the barrenness which had so happy an effect in the background of the picture, had advanced into the public house, which we expected to see smiling with a ripe harvest of rolls and cheese. This unlooked-for circumstance drove us again into our boat for we had quite outlived all the benefit derived from our foodful landlady at Combmartin.

9 LYNMOUTH

It was in 1812, just before Daniell and Ayton arrived, that the village was 'discovered' when Percy Bysshe Shelley sought temporary refuge here with his 16-year-old bride. In 1952 the village became front page news when the Lyn, 'who gives to the sea with great noise and pretension', and swollen with 24 hours of torrential rain, turned Ayton's comments into grim tragedy, sweeping away many buildings and claiming 34 lives. But the row of cottages in Daniell's view was untouched and remains to this day, with the Rising Sun Hotel being the principal property amongst them. The cottage where Shelley and his young bride stayed is behind the top house on the right and is a recent addition to the hotel's accommodation.

When Daniell and Ayton arrived at Minehead they were informed that there was '. . . nothing deserving of observation on this side of the Bristol Channel'. They, therefore, decided to cross over the sea to Cardiff and to commence their journey round the Welsh coast.

10 BRITTON FERRY

Britton Ferry forms a little haven at the mouth of the Neath, in the deepest recess of Swansea Bay, and is surrounded by scenery, which in richness and elegance I have seldom seen equalled in any other part of our coast. The river spreads at its confluence into a fine expanse of water, deep, smooth, and clear, and is bounded on each side by gentle hills, beautifully diversified in form, and covered with trees in full and stately growth.

The port of Britton Ferry is frequented principally by vessels employed in the service of the copper works and iron works of Neath. They bring copper ore from Cornwall and Anglesea; the iron ore and coals are obtained from mines at a short distance from the works.

10 BRITON FERRY

'The richness and elegance' described by Ayton disappeared long ago and industry, some of which is now in decay, has totally destroyed this scene. The bridge featured in my view and which was built in 1954, carries the A48 while, immediately above where I was sitting, the M4 straddles the Neath on a new bridge completed in 1995.

While working on this subject I was surrounded by ten of the most vicious youths, boys and girls, that I have ever seen. Threatening me with the vilest language and armed with sticks and stones, they forced me to retreat to the comparative safety of my car; it was with considerable difficulty and fear that I managed to escape a nasty situation, but not before the car had been damaged with stones in a number of places.

11 THE MUMBLES LIGHTHOUSE

Mumbles Head is a large, circular mass of rock gradually rising to a point and crowned with a lighthouse built in 1794. It is a handsome stone tower, sixty feet in height; the rock on which it stands is about the same height. The light is of very extensive utility, serving as a general guide for all vessels navigating this part of the Bristol Channel, which near the Welsh coast is obstructed by numerous shoals.

11 THE MUMBLES LIGHTHOUSE

The Swansea Harbour Trustees were given the power to provide a lighthouse at the outer Mumbles in the Harbour Act of 1791. In July 1792 the Trustees contracted for the erection of the lighthouse and work began; however, in October 1792 the half-finished structure collapsed. In 1793 the plans of a local architect were accepted and the lighthouse was finally completed and lit in 1794.

Mumbles Pier, together with the Pier Hotel, lie to the left of my view. The pier, built by the Widnes Foundry Company at a cost of £16,000, was opened on 10th May 1898. Originally a traditional pier with 'penny-in-the-slot' machines and Dodgem cars, it now has a helter-skelter, merry-go-rounds and video games. The hotel, which is non-residential and is on the mainland where the pier begins, is a popular discotheque.

12 WORM'S HEAD

Worm's Head derives its name from some resemblance which seamen have supposed it bears to a worm with its head erect, a simile which at least cannot be charged with the sin of exaggeration. In the spring and summer this promontory is covered with myriads of sea fowl: the most remarkable are the Eligugs, birds of passage of the Auk kind, and generally known by the name of the Razor-Bill. These birds seem to be exposed to no enemy but man, from whose rapacious invasions precipices cannot secure them. Places were pointed out to us to which people climbed in pursuit of a few eggs, which no combination of courage and caution could have enabled them to reach, but at imminent risk to their lives.

12 WORMS HEAD

Although there is a declivity near this view as depicted by Daniell, Worms Head cannot be seen from it. As on other occasions he has manipulated the subject for artistic effect; but this reminds me of a quotation by Oscar Wilde – 'No great artist ever sees things as they are. If he did he would cease to be an artist'. Much could be said and written about this observation but I do not intend to enter into a discourse on it at this stage of my 'Voyage'. For the moment I prefer to leave the reader to meditate on its significance.

In the spectacular sandy bay that sweeps northwards from Worms Head lie the skeletons of two nineteenth century shipwrecks, the City of Bristol and the Helvetia. Today, hang-gliders launch themselves off the stark cliff on the left of my view.

13 TENBY

There is something wild and romantic in the appearance of the town, rising abruptly from the sea, and mingling with all the ruggedness of the coast. It has been raised in the last twenty years from an obscure fishing town into a fashionable watering-place; it has one range of very good lodging-houses, a large hotel, and one of a subordinate character, and boasts among its more luxurious establishments a theatre and billiard room. The sudden accession of prosperity so inflated the minds of the natives, and so far intoxicated them, they lost all sense of moderation. Every article included in the requisitions of the visitors was raised to so monstrous a price, that they determined with one consent to abandon the place.

13 TENBY

The building at the end of the pier in Daniell's view was the old St Julian's Chapel for fishermen; converted into a bathing house in 1781, the structure was destroyed in 1842 when the pier was rebuilt. The sea-water baths at the left-hand end of the pier were completed in 1811 and Ayton comments that 'the building is very ornamental to the town ... with a reading room, copiously supplied with newspapers, and various publications on the benefits of bathing and the art of swimming'. The baths were later converted to a private residence called Laston House.

The spire is that of the church of St Mary, reputedly the largest church in Wales. Originally built in the early Norman period it was burnt down by the Welsh in 1186 and rebuilt by Warren de Munchensey, Earl of Pembroke, in 1245 with 14th, 15th and 16th century additions.

14 SOLVA

Solva, a small mean town, lies in a very romantic situation, at the bottom of a deep, narrow, and serpentine valley opening at the distance of half a mile into the sea. Nearer the sea, on the summit of a hill at the west side of the valley, there are six or eight cottages of rather more decent appearance, and these are called the Upper Town. A little wood on the side of the hills would make the little valley, with the sea winding through it, perfectly beautiful; but since the deluge, trees have refused to grow within sight of St Bride's Bay, and their place is here supplied by furze and fern.

14 SOLVA

Solva is a small, pleasant village with a sheltered harbour that was once busy with 30 or more coasters but is now mainly used as a safe anchorage for yachts and motor-boats.

The 'deluge' referred to by Ayton probably occurred in 1802 when the keeper of the nearby Smalls lighthouse, built in 1770, died during a violent storm. The assistant keeper lashed the body to a gangway until help could arrive, so that he could prove that the keeper's death had been an accident. It was three months before relief came, by which time he was half mad. Thereafter, the minimum crew for a lighthouse has always been three keepers but these have been superseded now by automation and there are no manned lighthouses today.

15 GOODWYCH PIER, FISHGUARD

In 1790, the Board of the Admiralty appointed a certain Mr Spence to make an estimate of the expenses that would be required for the erection of a proper pier. The survey was made, and the expenses estimated at £14,785 18s 6d but nothing further was done, and the harbour has at present only a very small pier, which is utterly inadequate for its protection.

Mr Spence clearly made out the advantages of Fishguard Bay and harbour which is formed by the estuary of the river Gwayn, and, unlike most harbours at the entrance to rivers, it has no bar, and is entirely free from all other obstructions.

15 GOODWICK PIER, FISHGUARD

This quiet scene depicted by Daniell was to become a terminal, built by the Great Western Railway, for transatlantic shipping sailing to New York but, although the liner Mauretania called at Goodwick in 1906, the long-distance sea trade soon shifted to Southampton, and the port settled down to a steady trade with Ireland.

The small building on the hill in Daniell's view is now the Fishguard Bay Hotel, which opened in the early years of the 20th century. At the time the tariff for a single room was 5/-, and you could have a fire in the morning or evening for 1/-. In recent years it has been used by film companies during the making of 'Moby Dick' and 'Under Milk Wood'.

16 VIEW NEAR ABERYSTWITH

The trade of Aberystwith, as far as the town is concerned, is trifling; but its port is the outlet for the produce of the surrounding country, which is very considerable. The interior of the harbour is well sheltered, but the entrance is exceedingly dangerous. This fact was brought home by the sight of a stranded vessel which had been wrecked in a gale. She was a Portuguese ship from Brazil, bound for Liverpool. The crew were still at Aberystwith where they were all crammed into a miserable kind of outhouse in a state of ineffable filth and wretchedness. Their lodging here was probably in no degree worse than in the forecastle of their vessel; but common humanity required that the inhabitants of the town should have given people, and especially foreigners, who had just escaped from the horrors of shipwreck, a more hospitable reception.

16 VIEW NEAR ABERYSTWYTH

This view is looking towards Tan-y-bwlch, a mansion at the foot of the hill from which the cliff acquired its name. Daniell's spelling of Aberystwith is the old form of the name and appears to reflect the difference in sound between the two 'y's; in Welsh the first is 'uh' and the second 'ih'.

The town is the home of the National Library of Wales which contains over two million volumes, with the world's largest collection of books in the Welsh language or relating to Wales. There is also an extensive collection of pictures (including four of mine) and maps. Daniell's chosen subject surprised me as there is a fine panoramic view from Constitution Hill that rises to the north of the town but I suspect that the presence of a wreck was too good an opportunity to be missed.

17 BARMOUTH

The town of Barmouth is the most singular in point of situation of any, and if it has any interest in the eyes of the traveller, must certainly derive it all from the whimsical inversion of every rule of comfort and convenience. It consists of four or five tiers of houses, ranged like the benches of a theatre on the side of a rocky hill, the chimneys of each tier being precisely on the same level as the doors of the tier above it. The houses at the lower range, which stand quite at the bottom of the hill, are the most respectable in appearance and, of course, are exempt from many of the evils which attach to their more airy neighbours; but their advantages are more than overbalanced by a high bank of sand before them, which not only intercepts their view of the sea, but sprightlily introduces itself in a west wind into every pervious cranny from the garrets to the ground.

17 BARMOUTH

Whenever possible I begin work in the early hours of the day so that, hopefully, if the weather deteriorates and rain sets in before noon, I will have produced something worthwhile. There are occasions, though, when my best intentions are defeated by the elements, and gloom and despondency become my companions. And so it was at Barmouth, where early showers developed into torrential downpours and the view before me gradually disappeared. With Daniell's habit of moving mountain ranges, I have no idea if his interpretation is correct, but I believe that his view was taken from the spit of land that stretches towards Barmouth from Fairbourne.

John Ruskin became associated with Barmouth in 1874 when he was given some old cottages so that he could practise his ideas of social reform on their inhabitants. The scheme, which was associated with his Guild of St George, was short-lived as he soon suffered a mental breakdown.

18 CAERNARVON

Caernarvon is very delightfully situated on the border of the Menai, which here assumes the character of a deep and placid river. The town is one of the largest in North Wales, and unquestionably one of the handsomest. The castle fills up nearly the whole of the southern front of the town and the vast mass of building makes every other castle in Wales quite insignificant. As we passed under its walls, its unguarded gateways at once checked all the wanderings of fancy; but, excepting some of the battlements, no other part of its exterior exhibited any material signs of damage or decay. There are no manufactories but the business of the port is extensive. The exports consist principally of slates, which are procured from a quarry seven miles to the eastward and shipped to London, Liverpool, Bristol and Dublin.

18 CAERNARFON

This view is from near a pleasant, small public house called the Mermaid Inn on Anglesey but Daniell has taken the liberty of moving a whole range of mountains in order to enhance his composition. I arrived here in the early hours of the morning, where I completed my drawing before the tantalising smell of a cooked breakfast enticed me into the inn. It was not long before I was well sustained for the rest of the day.

19 SOUTH STACK LIGHTHOUSE, HOLYHEAD

The two men who have charge of lighting and watching the lamps have a neat comfortable cottage on the island. One of the men has a wife who has filled the cottage with children, and the whole establishment presented a scene of social life and comfort. A year or two ago this little family was narrowly preserved from calamity. The children had wandered from the house to play, and scrambled into a small cart, lying near the east end of the island, which slopes down rapidly to the edge of the cliff: by romping about they put the cart in motion, when, from some sudden and strange impulse, for they were not alarmed or aware of their danger, they all jumped out, and escaped just before it was precipitated over the cliff and dashed to atoms.

19 SOUTH STACK LIGHTHOUSE, HOLYHEAD

The tiny islet known as South Stack Rock lies separated, by about 30 metres, from Holyhead Island where large granite cliffs rise sheer from the turbulent sea to a height of more than 60 metres. The lighthouse was originally envisaged in 1665 but it was not until 1809 that the first light, costing £12,000, was erected to mark the rock. About 1840, a railway was installed by means of which a lantern with a subsidiary light could be lowered down the cliff to sea level, when fog obscured the main light. In 1984 the lighthouse was automated and the keepers withdrawn.

My view is from the mainland where there is a fine walk up to Holyhead Mountain from which it is possible to see the Isle of Man and, in the right conditions, the mountains of Ireland.

20 THE HARBOUR LIGHTHOUSE, HOLYHEAD

The situation of Holyhead is singularly dreary and comfortless. The town is very small, consisting principally of one narrow and irregular street: the houses are mostly inhabited by poor people, and are, of course, small; but they may be remarked for their neatness and cleanliness. We found wretched accommodation in a large, dirty and ill-provided inn, which was much less annoying to our well seasoned and blunted feelings on such subjects, than it must prove to the weary and sea-sick passengers from Ireland. There is no trade of any kind in the place; but the continual influx of strangers brings money into it, and is the chief support of the inhabitants. There are seven packets at Holyhead, one of which sails every day, if not prevented by the weather. They are all fine, stout sloops, admirably appointed, and commanded by gentlemen of high respectability.

20 HOLYHEAD

A map of Holyhead Harbour, dated 1802, shows that the lighthouse depicted by Daniell was situated on Salt Island. All trace of it has disappeared under a new pier that was built in 1821, which incorporated the present lighthouse designed by the civil engineer, John Rennie. My view shows the Clock House on the left, with Admiralty Arch in approximately the position where the earlier lighthouse would have stood. The arch was erected to commemorate the opening of Thomas Telford's road from London, and the visit of George IV, who embarked at Holyhead for Ireland.

21 AMLWCH

As we approached Amlwch the country became still more barren and dreary: here all vegetation is blighted and tarnished by the poisonous fumes from the copper-works. About fifty years ago Amlwch was a village of six cottages, when it was suddenly raised to importance by the discovery of the great treasure in the Parys Mountain, and in a few years became the most considerable town in Anglesea. Nothing met our observation that bore the marks of cheerfulness and comfort: the streets were swarming with half-naked children, the men and women were equally ragged and filthy and their habitations looked black and ruinous. Many families have fled, and their cottages are now falling to ruin; but there is still a much more numerous population than can be supported by the mines and many are consequently in miserable destitution, unfitted for other employment or ignorant where to seek it.

21 AMLWCH

The port of Amlwch was built in 1793 to load the ships that took the copper ore, mined from nearby Parys Mountain, to destinations all over the world. The sloping, roofless buildings were storage bins for grain and were erected in the 1770s. Horse drawn carts would bring the grain to the harbour and it would be unloaded down wooden chutes into the bins. The square building was the Watchhouse Pier, which at one time had a fixed light to guide sailors into the port; this appears to have been part of a long series of port improvements organised under an Act of 1793, and was probably erected about 1853.

22 RED WHARF BAY

We suddenly found ourselves at Red Wharf, a capacious and beautiful bay, running several miles into the land. From an eminence near its western point, we had a grand panorama view of this deep inlet, with the country round it describing two-thirds of a vast circle. The picture was enlivened by some sloops and fishing boats, lying at anchor under the land, and by a small village scattered about at the water's edge. At low water the whole bed of the bay is left dry, and it becomes a wide desert of sand.

22 RED WHARF BAY

There was once a prosperous ship-building industry here, which built cargo vessels for Anglesey's copper-exporting trade; now only a row of cottages remains. A few leisure craft are moored in the wide, sandy bay where the tide ebbs and flows rapidly, sometimes stranding walkers who try to take a short cut.

A notable feature of Daniell's scenes is that the men all wear top hats, whether they are sitting quietly, leaning over the edge of a cliff or being tossed about in a boat.

23 BLACK MARBLE QUARRY

In arriving at Black Marble quarry, which lies on the north side of Red Wharf Bay, we were prevented from observing a few objects of mild interest by the impregnable obstinacy and stupidity of our guide. He had fixed upon a certain line of march in his own mind, entirely independent of our wishes, and he was not to be diverted from his course, either by threats or persuasion. His leading marks were public-houses, which he found out in succession as they occurred, with undeviating accuracy, becoming at each call more and more insensible to our anger and abuse. We remonstrated with him very vehemently for some time, but, at length, we gave up the contest as quite hopeless, and submitted to him as one who submits to the Solar System, or any other uncontrollable ordination.

23 BLACK MARBLE QUARRY

The licensee of the public house at Red Wharf Bay, where our intrepid travellers' guide may well have taken them, gave me directions to the quarry and I set off in the hope of finding some substantial remains of this industry. But all I could see was a small cottage. In an attempt to ascertain more precisely the location of the quarry, I approached a lady who had just come out of the door of the cottage. I showed her Daniell's engraving but she could not help – she was blind.

Eventually, I found a small outcrop of the black marble just behind the cottage. The rest had been used for building the pier at Holyhead in the early nineteenth century.

24 PUFFIN ISLAND

The island is rented from Lord Bulkeley by some poor people whose principal harvest is the Puffins, which, though robbed year after year, seem to make their annual return in undiminished numbers. It is only the young birds that are of any value, and these are prized for their down and their flesh, though the latter requires a very elaborate expurgation before it can be freed from its rankness. They were set before us at Beaumaris as a delicacy, but they that would eat them pickled should never look upon them alive. When my friend had finished his sketch, and dotted it with Puffins till he was tired, we made a tour round the island. It was almost low water when we left, and there was a tremendous surf upon the causeway, but we were in the way of only the last tier of breakers, and escaped with a sprinkling.

24 PUFFIN ISLAND

The island, formerly called Priestholm, derives its English name from the large colonies of puffins which still breed here. At one time there were much larger groups but these were decimated by rats, and by local inhabitants who found pickled puffin to be a tasty delicacy. I decided not to visit the island, for which permission has to be obtained, but to depict the view from the mainland.

The lighthouse, called Black Point, or Tywyn-Du, was established in 1838 at a cost of £11,589 and originally manned by two keepers. However, these were withdrawn in 1922 when the lighthouse was converted to unwatched acetylene operation.

The island owes its Welsh name of Ynys Seiriol to the saint who established a monastic settlement there 14 centuries ago.

25 BEAUMARIS

Beaumaris castle, the last erected by Edward I in Wales, is in no respect to be compared with his magnificent castles of Caernarvon and Conway. It covers a great extent of ground but the whole building is so disproportionately low, that, when seen but from a very short distance, it appears a heavy, sunken, and unvaried mass, without either dignity or elegance.

Beaumaris has many visitors in the summer season and there is no spot in the kingdom that offers more attraction to those who have any perception of what is beautiful, picturesque, and sublime in nature.

25 BEAUMARIS

This was a difficult subject to portray, as the castle 'melted' into the background of trees and buildings. By chance, a passing cloud cast its shadow in such a way that, for a short while, the castle appeared to be all on its own with the Chapel of Rest in the middle distance on the right.

As early as 1822 English tourists were being offered excursions from Liverpool to Beaumaris and the pier, which was built in 1846, was improved in 1873, so that steamers could berth there; it is now shorter and used mainly for fishing parties or for trips to Puffin Island.

26 LADY PENRHYN'S BATH, NEAR BANGOR

This elegant little building, designed by James Wyatt, was constructed at an immense expense. The bath has much the character of an Italian building, and has a very happy effect on the border of this charming bay. It stands at the extremity of a road, carried out about two hundred and twenty yards into the strait, raised nearly thirty feet above the level of the water, and terminating in a circle, large enough to permit a carriage to turn around.

26 LADY PENRHYN'S BATH

I approached this subject from Penrhyn Harbour, and it was a long walk over a rocky foreshore which would soon be covered by the rising tide. The bath was built about 1808. In a book recording his journeys through North Wales, the Rev. W. Bingley describes the bath as a 'plain but elegant building, entered through a portico, fronted by four columns, which admits carriages to pass underneath. The baths are circular, one open at the top . . . being apparently about 30 feet in diameter; and a small one that will allow of the water being heated. The latter is within the building, and is lined with white and cream-coloured earthen-ware: under the window is a large and beautiful oval of the same, with a wreath of oak leaves within the rim, and a coronet with Lady Penrhyn's initials in the centre'.

The baths were used for target practice by the Bangor Home Guard during the Second World War. There are no plans to restore the building.

27 PENMAEN-MAWR TAKEN FROM NEAR ABER

We found a very comfortable little inn at Aber, which induced us to halt there for the night, and on the following morning we started for Conway. A fine level road leads for several miles from the village, through a delightful plain, bounded by Penmaen-Mawr, which now became the grand object of our attention. On arriving at its base, I determined, while my friend proceeded to Conway, to ascend to its summit.

27 PENMAENMAWR

A favourite holiday resort of Mr Gladstone, Penmaenmawr is dominated by 'the large stone head' from where the tough rock has found a ready market since prehistoric times. Ayton possibly ascended the same trail that leads visitors today to the site of a Stone Age axe factory, whose stone tools have been found as far apart as Wiltshire and Northern Ireland.

My view is taken farther away than Daniell's as I wanted to incorporate Great Orme which, in my youth, I explored during school holidays. At that time, steam trains were a great attraction in an area where Robert Stephenson had performed wonderous feats of engineering for the Chester and Holyhead Railway.

28 CONWAY

The town is entered through a grand gateway, but a minute's walk after passing this barrier puts to flight all thoughts of pomp and pride, and all objects, streets, houses and people, conspire to assure you that you are in one of the meanest and filthiest of Welsh towns. There is a tolerable inn, the only thing in modern Conway that can gratify a traveller. When seen from without, the appearance of the town is extremely beautiful and picturesque.

Conway ferry has called forth many a peevish paragraph from indignant tourists. but I shall not add my voice to the chorus as there is the prospect of the construction of a bridge. Mr Telford proposes to throw a cast iron arch of two hundred feet across the water and the expense of the work is estimated at £44,178.

28 CONWY

At one time, the narrow streets of Conwy were a major obstacle to holiday traffic as it crawled along the North Wales coast. Telford's elegant but narrow bridge, opened in 1826, remained the only means of crossing the river until the modern road bridge was opened in 1958. But this only increased the density of traffic until, in 1991, the town was by-passed by a tunnel under the mouth of the river. A third bridge, designed by Robert Stephenson and completed in 1849, carries the railway in two rectangular tubes side by side, each 130 metres long, and resting at one end on balls and rollers.

I had no difficulty in finding Daniell's viewpoint, which is between Llandudno Junction and Deganwy, but it will be seen that the mountain range behind the castle is totally different.

With my visit to Conwy, I completed the third stage of my Voyage in October 1991.

29 LIGHTHOUSE ON THE POINT OF AIR

As we stood at the foot of the lighthouse we were much struck with the dreary aspect of this dismal shore. The sea had ebbed far out, leaving exposed a desert of sand, at least a mile in breadth and extending in length as far as the eye could reach. On the sands were strewed about pieces of wreck and heaps of stranded fish; and not far from us lay the whitened skeleton of a horse, which looked a huge strange thing, and had a good effect in this picture of desolation.

The lighthouse has two windows in the light-room, one shewing a light to the eastward to the river Dee, and the other pointing to the W.N.W as a guide over Chester Bar.

29 LIGHTHOUSE ON THE POINT OF AYR

This was not exactly the most exciting place to begin the fourth stage of my Voyage but, no doubt, it was chosen by my predecessor because the subject is primarily a lighthouse. I, too, saw it under circumstances 'particularly favourable to its dreariness' and my sentiments were much the same. Although there was no skeleton of a horse, the presence of several youths on motorbikes was equally disturbing – and it began to rain.

The approach to the sands, which lie on the south side of the Dee estuary, is through holiday camps and caravan sites. The lighthouse has not been in use since 1883 and is now in private ownership. Unfortunately, it is slowly tilting over and the owner has had to pour large quantities of concrete under its base in an effort to prevent a total collapse.

30 SEACOMBE FERRY, LIVERPOOL

From Seacombe Ferry, Liverpool appeared to great advantage on the opposite coast, with such a grove of masts extended before it as could be seen, perhaps, London excepted, in no other port in the world. Behind the shipping rose a range of vast warehouses, which concealed from us the great body of the town, but its extent was indicated by the wide-spreading atmosphere of smoke. This was certainly the most noble and animating sight that we had seen during our tour, not only grand and picturesque, but possessing a high moral interest, as it brought before our minds the country in the pride of its industry and enterprise, and under the most striking signs of its wealth, consequence and power.

30 SEACOMBE FERRY, LIVERPOOL

Daniell and Ayton visited Liverpool in the autumn of 1814. When I arrived here in September 1993, the east bank of the Mersey was barely visible and it certainly could not be seen 'to great advantage'. The rain that curtailed my visit to the Point of Ayr had intensified, and the situation reminded me of the start of my Voyage in 1988 when a similar downpour almost made me give up the whole project. But, eventually, patience was rewarded and the rain eased off long enough to enable me to sit near the ferry terminal to do the necessary drawing.

The waterfront buildings of Liverpool are well known and most of these survived the air raids of the Second World War. Regrettably, though, the 'picturesque' scene has not been improved by the late 20th century developments.

31 LIVERPOOL

The public buildings of Liverpool are striking monuments of the liberal and munificent spirit of its inhabitants. Here are no appearances of meanness or parsimony; every building is quite complete, and fully adapted to the purposes for which it was designed, with an addition of embellishment, which shews that the founders were not only ready to do all that was required, but to do it in the handsomest manner. Great neatness, cleanliness, and liveliness of appearance, characterize the greater part of the town in its fashionable and most busy quarters; but there is a considerable proportion of close and filthy alleys and lanes to be seen, though so situated that they need not be found out by one walking to admire only the most agreeable objects of the place.

31 LIVERPOOL

Ayton found an abundance of matter in Liverpool to occupy him fully and pleasantly, during a week of observation. But Daniell had exhausted all that it presented of the picturesque in a much shorter time and proceeded on his tour. I found the streets of Birkenhead particularly depressing and the docks had virtually disappeared. It was not possible to go window-shopping after closing hours, as most shops hid behind steel shutters. Apartment blocks, with views of the lifeless river, have replaced the warehouses, and it was from the car park of one of these that I did this view of Liverpool. The drawing took about two hours to complete but, to my dismay, I found that it was on the back of the drawing for no. 30. This was most frustrating as both subjects were particularly difficult to do, and such carelessness is an annoying waste of time.

32 VIEW NEAR LOWER HEYSHAM

A man fond of poring over old tombstones (and who is not?) may be pleased to muse for an hour in the church-yard here. The church, which is very small, has suffered much from modern alterations, but still retains a trace of its antiquity, in a Saxon arch forming the entrance. There is nothing observable within it; but many tombstones, and fragments of them, are evidently of no modern date. Nearby there is a ruined chapel dedicated to St Patrick and, alongside, there are six curious coffins in a row, hollowed out in the rock, with the head and general form of the body defined. They are all nearly of an equal size, and were designed for persons of small stature.

32 OLD HEYSHAM

These curious graves probably date from the 8th-9th century. There has been considerable erosion since Daniell's visit; all the walls depicted in his view have disappeared and the sides of the graves are well rounded.

I had arrived late in the day at the village of Old Heysham and, with rain threatening again, I started drawing the subject immediately. In so doing I had delayed looking for accommodation for the night and this proved difficult to find. Daniell and his companion also had similar problems and it was not unusual for them to face the prospect of having to share a bed with two or three evil-smelling partners. Eventually, I found a small guest-house where a jolly evening was spent in the company of ten other residents who had visited the same establishment for many years. Fortunately, I had my bedroom to myself.

33 LANCASTER

Our arrival at Lancaster coincided with the commencement of the assizes and it was necessary for us to look about with as much dispatch as possible; as the coming of the judges would make a bed an accommodation not to be thought of by any one who had not laid his plans a month beforehand. The hurry and confusion had already begun, in preparation for the business of the sessions, and the general festival out of prison, which takes place on the trial of the wretches within. It is rather too much to see the ladies putting on their bonnets in the morning, to look at the judges and hear the prisoners condemned to death; and then take them off again, to prepare for the dance at night; one may be permitted to feel something revolting in the very name of the 'assize-ball'.

33 LANCASTER

Lancashire is renowned for its rainfall but, after my visit to Old Heysham, the deluge that followed that night was exceptional. As often happens, though, the morning dawned bright and clear and I hastened to Lancaster where I was able to complete a quick sketch before the next downpour.

Daniell's view shows only the castle and the church, whereas today there is considerable unsympathetic development in the foreground. To the left, but out of sight, are the railway and road bridges across the River Lune. In the distance is the dome of the Ashton Memorial, built in 1909 by Lord Ashton in memory of his wife.

The castle has been a courthouse and prison for centuries and in 1612 ten Lancashire witches were convicted and hanged within its precincts.

34 CASTLE HEAD

Castle Head is a singular crag, rising precipitously from the water, and crowned with a luxuriant thicket of wood, amidst which is seen some little ornamental building, which, with scraps of the path and railing leading to it, has a very pretty effect. At its base, close upon the shore, stands an elegant villa with a line of trees, at the water's edge, skreening it on one side, and the grounds about it embellished with every tasteful addition practical in the situation. The mansion struck me as a most delightful and inviting habitation.

34 CASTLE HEAD

The mansion was built about 1780 by the ironfounder and furnaceman, John Wilkinson; it was he who assisted James Watt in the development of the steam engine. One of the conditions of the purchase of the property was that he had to build a sea bank across the valley in the winter of 1778-1779 and this is shown in Daniell's view; but Daniell visited Castle Head in 1814 and water still remains in the foreground of his picture.

Wilkinson died in 1808 and, in Daniell's view, the cast iron monument to him can be seen on the cliff; this was re-erected in later years in the nearby village of Lindale. The bridge on the left of my view was built by Wilkinson and is surmounted by one of the earliest examples of wrought-iron railings. The property is now the Castle Head Field Centre.

35 PEEL CASTLE

The castle was built by an abbot of Furness Abbey, probably as a place of shelter for the brotherhood, and the wealth of the abbey, in case of any attack on it; and great art and labour was employed in order to render it a secure one. Two sides of the castle stand at the edge of a steep bank, immediately above the sea; and the sides towards the land are defended by two walls of great thickness, each flanked with square towers surrounded by a ditch. In a space between the outer and inner wall, or, to speak classically, within the outer ballium, was a small chapel, now only to be traced in its foundations. There is a public house nearby inhabited by an old Scotchman who is supported by donations from occasional seafarers in the summer time; he acknowledged that when there were no vessels in the roadstead he was apt to be driven to his beer-barrel for company.

35 PIEL CASTLE

Barrow-in-Furness came as a complete surprise to me with its sprawling development, docks and large ship-building hangars. To find the viewpoint of the castle it was necessary to reach the southern tip of the Isle of Walney. I arrived late in the afternoon, only to discover that I had to pass through a nature reserve, which had closed for the rest of the day. The approach was through a depressing housing estate, followed by a sad-looking holiday camp; then a long walk over the beach to find the view.

When I returned the next morning, there was again the threat of rain, and I had to make a quick sketch of the castle. The general outline is still very much as Daniell found it, although he makes the roadstead much narrower. A ballium, referred to by Ayton, is the outer wall of a feudal castle.

36 WHITEHAVEN

Whitehaven owes its rise entirely to the Lowther family, who, by the extensive scale on which they have worked their valuable mines of coal, have advanced it, within a hundred and twenty years, from an obscure hamlet to its present size and consequence. It now contains about fifteen thousand inhabitants, and the number is continually increasing. Ship-building is carried on here to a considerable extent and there are two hundred and four vessels belonging to the port. Of this number sixty-two vessels are employed in foreign commerce while the remainder are engaged entirely in the exportation of coals.

36 WHITEHAVEN

The pier, as depicted by Daniell, with the small building and tower at its end, still exists. Today, though, there is no 'exportation of coals' from Whitehaven and, like other towns in the area, the population of 26,000 now relies heavily on the Sellafield nuclear fuel reprocessing plant and the Marchon chemical works for its livelihood. The building in the middle distance of Daniell's view is the above ground workings of William Pit coal mine, and the two chimneys in the distance are the 'Tobacco Pipes'; these and their associated range of buildings were used for the storage and destruction of contraband tobacco until they were demolished in 1923.

Daniell and Ayton had been travelling together for two years and it was at Whitehaven that there appear to be the first signs of discontent. Ayton wrote '. . . I pursued my journey alone as my friend's time was too valuable to him to make such frequent and long pauses as my more multifarious concerns made it necessary for me to do'.

37 MARYPORT

The largest and most respectable part of the town is pleasantly situated on high ground; it is well built, and regularly laid out, the houses neat and the streets airy and spacious; but the lower division is as wretched as may be, betraying a condition of shabbiness and filthiness.

The harbour of Maryport is very small, and ill-suited to the wealth and commercial importance of the place; it is protected against the swell of the sea by two wooden breakwaters which shew by various gaps and fractures the insufficiency of the materials of which they are composed. Violent remonstrances have been made to the lord of the manor by the ship-owners concerning the inconvenience and insecurity of the harbour, but he has not attended to them, and some of them have consequently left the port.

37 MARYPORT

Once a bustling port with over 140 trading vessels, Maryport is now a haven for pleasure craft, a few fishing boats and a selection of preserved vessels. Some apartment blocks have been built around the docks, and areas of brick roads and pavings are waiting for further residential development, which show little sign of materialising.

The harbour was built in the 18th century by a Mr Senhouse and named after his wife, Mary. The principal trade at the time was the export of coal, and the wooden breakwaters that caused so much concern at the time of Daniell's visit, are shown on the left of his view. The pier on the right is in approximately the same position as the pier in my view, on which the derelict harbour light is standing.

38 CAERLAVEROCK CASTLE

There are few remains of castles like this in Scotland. Once the seat of the Maxwells, I have seen none comparable with it. Its grandeur is purely its own, for it is in a very bad situation, at least for the purposes of show, standing on a flat, from which it cannot be seen to advantage from any distance. The ground, however, is improved by some fine trees, which give a gloom and solemnity to it, harmonising with the antiquity and the ruinousness of the building.

38 CAERLAVEROCK CASTLE

And so, at long last, I reached Scotland for the first time. This castle made a pleasant subject on which to begin the long journey round the coast of Scotland and the Western Isles. There has been little change to this scene, although the trees behind the castle are taller, thus obscuring the view of the sea and Cumbria.

I was not sure what to expect when I crossed the border, but everything and everybody seemed much the same as south of the border. However, Ayton commented – 'that whisky is the favourite drink of the people is very evident, not only from the prevalence of red noses, but from a direct notice that it is to be bought at every other house in the place. We perceived a 'draper and dealer in spirits, a grocer and dealer in spirits', and an even more extraordinary union, a 'banker and dealer in spirits'.

39 KIRKCUDBRIGHT

Kirkcudbright is a very small town, consisting principally of two short streets, neat, clean and quiet, without manufacture, and with very limited commercial relations beyond its own immediate vicinity. It contains nothing that can claim the notice of a traveller, except an old castle, and that is interesting only from its antiquity.

Having enjoyed some rest and refreshment, I crossed the ferry and continued my journey. Ferryboats and fares are in general so justly the objects of a traveller's indignation and reproaches, that I must mention the admirable appointment of the boat at this place, and the extreme moderation of the fare. The charge for a man is a half-penny, and for a horse a penny. The boat runs along a rope stretched across the river, and is pushed along by a single person, with great ease and expedition.

39 KIRKCUDBRIGHT

Dull, grey clouds hung around all day as I struggled with this view. It was not possible to sit in the same position as Daniell and I had to park myself in an uncomfortable place on the road bridge, which was undergoing major repairs. The noise of pneumatic drills and the constant stopping and starting of traffic were most irritating. The 16th-century McLellan's Castle has been partially restored and the white building on the waterfront is the Harbour Art Gallery.

My initial attempt to find accommodation for my first night in Scotland was not very successful. After driving up a long, dark track, I came upon a gaunt, dilapidated mansion that professed to provide bed and breakfast. I peered through a window where a smouldering fire cast grotesque shadows on the walls. For some reason, I turned away and fled, my imagination running riot.

40 CARDONESS CASTLE

Formerly the seat of the McCullocks, the castle stands on a high mount and consists of one square tower – a specimen of the utmost plainness that masonry can admit of. It must be remembered that these simple castles were not national fortresses, designed for the reception of regular troops, but were the houses merely of private individuals, built with the strength of castles as defence against violence and plunder. They give great interest to the country, calling up the memory of other times, with all the turbulence, danger, and distrust, as a contrast to the peacefulness and confidence of the days we live in. These castles are mostly very entire; and as they offer nothing to tempt rapacity, they may stand for ages to come, the memorials of a hateful state of life no doubt, but graced with a spirit of boldness and enterprise which captivates romantic imagination.

40 CARDONESS CASTLE

I expect to see many similar castles to this one during my travels round Scotland. Ayton commented that '. . . in spite of its exceeding rudeness, when seen from a little distance, and combined with the scenery of a picturesque bay, it is a good object, possessing the interest of evident antiquity, and not without some appearance of dignity'. A 15th-century castle, it is one of the best preserved of its period in Scotland and notable for its elaborate fireplaces.

The 'picturesque bay' has receded and the A75 cuts right across the valley and over the Water of Fleet. As on previous occasions, Daniell has made the hills in the background more prominent, but he does include a feature that does not appear in any of the other scenes of his Voyage – a hay wagon.

41 WIGTON

Wigton is a small decent town, situated near the mouth of a stream, on an eminence at a considerable elevation from the sea. In this respect it differs from the small towns on the coast, which are generally situated in valleys. It commands a very striking and extensive view of the bay. The scarcity of fuel is one of its great disadvantages; peat, which is the only kind consumed here, is procured from a tract in the neighbourhood, which bears all the marks of having been once covered by the sea. The tract must have been covered with wood, as trunks of trees are still found in great numbers interspersed through the whole of it. They are mostly oak and they lie in such a direction as if they had yielded to the force of the west wind, which is most violent in these districts.

41 WIGTOWN

From Wigtown onwards Daniell was now on his own. There is no suggestion of a rift between the two travellers but, from my own experience, an artist can find it difficult to work alongside someone else for any length of time.

The present view of Wigtown is rather different from that depicted by Daniell, the sea having receded to leave an extensive area of tidal sands, saltings and marshland. Had Ayton still been on the Voyage he may well have commented on the foul act in the history of Wigtown Bay when, in 1685, two woman Covenanters aged 18 and 65, who had refused to change their religious allegiance, were tied to stakes and left to be drowned by the rising tide.

42 THE MULL OF GALLOWAY

The Mull of Galloway is a rugged and rather lofty headland and is unfortunately destitute of a lighthouse, though the measure of erecting one has been repeatedly suggested. A more rocky coast is rarely to be found than that which extends between the Mull of Galloway and Port Nessick. The project of building a pier at this port has for some time been in agitation, the situation as a harbour being considered preferable in every respect to Port Patrick.

42 THE MULL OF GALLOWAY

A severe gale was blowing when I arrived at this desolate peninsula and it was with considerable difficulty that I found the viewpoint; fortunately the wind was blowing off the sea, otherwise I could have ended up at the bottom of the cliffs.

This southernmost tip of Scotland was not 'destitute of a lighthouse' for very long after Daniell's visit, as the present structure was erected in 1830. Port Nessick, mentioned by Daniell, was Port Nessock but today it is called Port Logan.

43 DUNSKEY CASTLE

About a mile to the southward of Port Patrick stand the ruins of Dunskey Castle, on the brink of a precipice whose base is washed by the sea. It seems to have been well constructed for defence, and exhibits some remains of embankments on the land side, which shew it to have been a handsome building. The access to it was over a drawbridge. In the neighbourhood of the castle there is a cave for which the people have a very superstitious regard, as being favourable to cure infirm persons, particularly of rickety children.

43 DUNSKEY CASTLE

I continued my battle against the elements with a visit, late in the day, to this 15th-century castle. It is approached by paths along the edge of the cliff or along the old railway track. The scene is similar to Daniell's view in which he has shown the coast of Northern Ireland, but this was obscured by low cloud and drizzle during my visit.

The castle is not as isolated as it may appear; just to its right there is a large park for caravans and tents.

44 PORT PATRICK

The harbour was originally a mere inlet between two ridges of rocks. The coast of Ireland lies right in front at a distance of about twenty miles. Regular intercourse between Port Patrick and Donaghadee could only be maintained when the winds were northerly or southerly and it was therefore desirable that the harbour should be rendered capable of protecting vessels, properly constructed for sailing at all points. This object was accomplished about the year 1774, by the late Mr Smeaton. These improvements, with the addition of a lighthouse, have tended greatly to facilitate the passage of vessels between this place and the north of Ireland.

44 PORTPATRICK

This was a pleasant place to stay and to sketch. Despite the improvements to the port mentioned by Daniell, the harbour proved to be too small and exposed for the increase in shipping, which was eventually moved farther north to Stranraer.

The public toilets were to the right of where I was sitting; such places are not usually noteworthy but these were the most agreeable that I have ever visited. They were spotlessly clean with fresh flowers, colourful soaps, perfume, clean towels and with such a delicate decor that one might be excused for mistaking them for conveniences in a five star hotel.

45 THE CRAG OF AILSA

This noted and valuable landmark is said to be from 800 to 900 feet high, and, being insular, the abruptness and singularity of its form render its appearance very striking. The island is not inhabited by any human being, but affords refuge to immense flocks of solan geese and other sea-birds.

45 AILSA CRAIG

There must have been a sea mist at the time of Daniell's visit, as the Isle of Arran, which is clearly visible from this viewpoint at Ballantrae, is not shown in his aquatint. The Craig itself seems to be smaller than he has depicted but, in conversation with a local inhabitant, I learnt that its appearance can vary considerably depending on the light and the state of the tide.

Salmon and lobster fishing is the main activity here now. The pier was built in 1852 and the large building on the right is the former lifeboat house, which was closed in 1917.

46 CULZEAN CASTLE

Culzean Castle, the residence of the Earl of Cassilis, is situated on the verge of an almost perpendicular rock, the height of which from the sea is about 100 feet. The plan of the present edifice was furnished by the late Mr Adam. Few situations comprehend a greater variety of picturesque scenery. From the principal apartments there is a fine view of the isles of Arran, Pladda, Holy Island, with the whole of the Firth of Clyde, in the midst of which rises the bold and abrupt Crag of Ailsa.

46 CULZEAN CASTLE

I had been looking forward to drawing this subject ever since I first saw Daniell's view of it. Designed by Robert Adam and completed in 1790 around an ancient tower belonging to the Kennedy family, the castle is now owned by the National Trust for Scotland; its name is pronounced 'cullane'.

The approach to Daniell's viewpoint is down a steep flight of steps and then along the foreshore. But Ailsa Craig can only just be seen behind the cliffs on which the castle stands, whereas Daniell has made it much more prominent. Just to the left of the view there is a small, private gas works, which was one of the earliest examples of the commercial use of gas.

There is now a Country Park in the grounds of the castle, with a Visitor Centre in the Home Farm complex of buildings, which were also designed by Robert Adam.

47 DISTANT VIEW OF AYR

Grinean Castle, a most singular ruin, stands on the summit of a rock rising abruptly from the sea, not far from the heads of Ayr. From this place the town of Ayr has a respectable appearance. It is situated on a level peninsula formed by the converging rivers Ayr and Doon, which here flow into the sea. The river is embellished by several good bridges, and in the principal street, which is wide, there are some well built houses.

47 DISTANT VIEW OF AYR

Standing dramatically on the edge of the cliff, Greenan Castle remains unchanged and, despite its precarious siting, shows no sign of collapse. The approach is through a housing estate, where one signpost pointed directly at a private house – a small but annoying inconvenience not only for me but, more so, for the owner.

Now that Daniell was travelling alone, he had to carry out his own research into the history of the places he visited and this must have become an enormous undertaking. His text is less detailed than Ayton's, which covered the social conditions and historical facts in greater depth, but Daniell does describe, with reasonable accuracy, the positions of most of his viewpoints, which has made my task a little easier.

48 VIEW OF STEAM BOATS ON THE CLYDE, NEAR DUMBARTON

In proceeding from Greenock up to Dumbarton, a conveyance offered itself which forms a very striking peculiarity in the navigation of the Clyde. This was the steam-boat, of which a sufficient number have been established to maintain a constant intercourse between Greenock and Glasgow. They can depart at any time of the tide and in all winds, and perform the voyage in generally three hours. The smoke of the engine is carried off by a tall cast-iron chimney, bearing the semblance of a mast. The principal cabin for passengers is furnished with draught and chess boards, back-gammon tables, and other implements of pastime, as well as with a small library of that description of books denominated light reading; on the roof there are chairs and benches for the convenience of those who, in fine weather, choose to enjoy the delightful prospects on both shores of the Clyde.

48 NEAR DUMBARTON

During the 19th century, Port Glasgow was the principal Scottish port handling timber for shipbuilding. Logs were fastened together and floated to storage pools where they were seasoned by salt water until needed. The pools were square or rectangular and were rented from landowners but, with the advent of iron- and steel-hulled vessels, the use of timber declined. By 1914 few timber pools were still in use but, at low tide, the stakes which enclosed them can still be seen.

The view is from almost the same place as Daniell's – through some playing fields on the north side of the A8 – and the steamboat depicted by him is very similar to the 'Comet', launched in 1812 at Port Glasgow, a replica of which stands in a car park in the centre of the town.

I came to the end of this fourth stage of my Voyage on 19th September 1994. With the weather fine and settled it was tempting to cross the Clyde and to begin my exploration of the Western Isles, where the Isle of Arran stood out boldly against a setting sun. But, for the time being, it was necessary to return home and to prepare for adventures elsewhere . . .

INDEX